BRANDON
GOES TO
HONG KONG

BRANDON GOES TO HONG KONG (香港 Xiānggǎng)

Eugenia Chu

Illustrated by Eliza Hsu Chen

Brandon Goes to Hong Kong (Xiānggǎng 香港)
All Rights Reserved
Copyright © 2021 Eugenia Chu
Miami, Florida

The opinions expressed in this manuscript are solely the opinions of the author. The author has represented and warranted full ownership and/or legal right to publish all the materials in this book.

All rights reserved. No part of this publication may be reproduced, distributed, or transmitted in any form or by any means, including photocopying, recording, or other electronic or mechanical methods, without the prior written permission of the publisher, except in the case of brief quotations embodied in critical reviews and certain other noncommercial uses permitted by copyright law.

ISBN-13: 978-1-7334808-1-9

Library of Congress Control Number: 2021902197

Illustrated by: Eliza Hsu Chen

First printing edition 2021

www.eugeniachu.com

To Brandon and Kelsey.
May your imaginations take you far.

CONTENTS

	Preface	1
1.	Arriving in Hong Kong—*Xiānggǎng* (香港)	4
2.	Surprise Visitors	6
3.	Meeting Kelsey	11
4.	Lantau Island and the Big Buddha (Sunday)	15
5.	Victoria Peak (Monday)	22
6.	Victoria Harbour Symphony of Lights	25
7.	Researching Dragons: Part 1	30
8.	Ocean Park (Tuesday)	32
9.	Real Live Dragons	39
10.	Dinner with Kelsey	46
11.	Hong Kong Disneyland (Wednesday)	48
12.	Researching Dragons: Part 2	51

13. Researching Dragons: Part 3 (Thursday)	56
14. Star Ferry and Kowloon; Mid-Levels Escalator	58
15. Last Night in *Xiānggǎng* (香港)	62
16. The Dream?	65
17. Going Home (Friday)	70
Glossary	74
Notes	79
About the Author	80
About the Illustrator	81

PREFACE

This book contains a few words and phrases written in Chinese characters (Simplified) and spelled in Pinyin.

Unlike English (and other Roman-based languages), where each letter in each word represents a sound, Chinese writing evolved from pictures and symbols. Chinese characters represent words and do not constitute an alphabet or represent sounds. Accordingly, Pinyin is often used by those learning Chinese.

Pinyin is the official system to transcribe Mandarin Chinese sounds into the Roman alphabet. It was invented in the 1950s, and adopted as a standard in mainland China in 1958. Pinyin assigns letters different sounds. For example:

> **ai** is pronounced as *i* in *like*
> **ao** is pronounced as *ow* in *how*
> **iao** is pronounced as *eow* in *meow*
> **iang** is pronounced as *young*
> **ie** is pronounced as *ye* in *yes*
> **iu** is pronounced as *yo* in *yolk*
> **ui** is pronounced as *way*

Eugenia Chu

In addition, in Mandarin Chinese there are four basic tones and a fifth neutral tone.* Each syllable in each word has one of these tones. Changing the tone of a word changes its meaning. You can tell which tone to give a syllable by the marks above the vowels in pinyin (¯ ′ ˇ `).

The first tone is high and remains level.
It is represented by : ▬

The second tone goes up and is abrupt.
It is represented by : ╱

The third tone falls in pitch and then goes up again.
It is represented by : ∨

The fourth tone falls in pitch from a high to a low level.
It is represented by : ╲

There is also a neutral (or toneless) tone, which is pronounced weakly. The neutral tone has no mark above the vowel.

Chinese is a fun language to learn! I hope you will enjoy reading this story as much as I have enjoyed writing it.

---

*You can find a short video tutorial on pronunciation and tones on my website at www.eugeniachu.com.

Brandon Goes to Hong Kong (Xiānggǎng 香港)

This is Brandon—a 9 ¾ year old, smart and adventurous boy!

CHAPTER 1

Arriving in Hong Kong— *Xiānggǎng* (香港)

(Saturday)

After what seemed like an eternity of planning, packing, counting down the days and then traveling from their home in Miami, Brandon and his parents were finally landing in Hong Kong—*Xiānggǎng* (香港)! Brandon was all smiles as the plane was descending.

"Almost there!"

Brandon Goes to Hong Kong (Xiānggǎng 香港)

A flash of red swooshed by his window! Brandon turned to get a better look, but it was gone.

"Whoa, what was that? It definitely wasn't an airplane. Too big to be a bird. So strange..."

Brandon decided to keep this observation to himself, since he really had no idea what he had seen. It could have been nothing. Maybe it was jet lag causing him to imagine things. After all, *Xiānggǎng* (香港) was twelve hours ahead of Miami, so even though it was morning here in *Xiānggǎng* (香港), it felt like night time to Brandon!

What kind of adventures will Brandon have in Hong Kong—Xiānggǎng (香港)? What do you think the red swoosh was? Anything?

CHAPTER 2

Surprise Visitors

As they were arriving at the hotel, Mom turned around and looked at Brandon with a huge smile.

"What?" asked Brandon suspiciously, "Why are you smiling at me like that?"

Mom gave Dad a knowing look and then turned back to Brandon. "There's a surprise waiting for you at the hotel!"

"What? What is it—*Shì shénme* (是什么)?" cried Brandon as he enthusiastically jumped out of the car and followed his parents to the lobby of the hotel, which was huge and smelled like flowers.

Before they had a chance to answer, Brandon's Grandpa—*Gōnggong* (公公) and Grandma—*Pópo* (婆婆)[1], stepped out from around the corner.

"What—*Shénme* (什么)? How—*Zěnme* (怎么)?" Brandon was flabbergasted as he was smothered with hugs from *Gōnggong* (公公) and *Pópo* (婆婆). "I can't believe you guys are here! How awesome—*Tài bàng le* (太棒了)!"

For the rest of the day, Brandon and his family relaxed at the hotel while trying to both rest and simultaneously stay awake to overcome jet lag. Dad saw Brandon's eyes start to get heavy and immediately tossed Brandon his bathing suit.

Brandon yipped, quickly changed and headed to the pool on the roof of the hotel with his parents. Brandon smelled the chlorine even before opening the door to the pool—he inhaled deeply. That smell always brought back memories of fun times playing with his friends in the pool.

When he got to the pool, *Gōnggong* (公公) and *Pópo* (婆婆) were already there.

---

[1] *Gōnggong* (公公) means Grandpa (mother's father), which is short for *wàigōng* (外公) (grandfather); *Pópo* (婆婆) means Grandma (mother's mother), which is short for *wàipo* (外婆) (grandmother). Please see the Glossary for more names of family members in Chinese.

"How do they always appear out of nowhere?" Brandon wondered as he joined them in the cool water at the shallow end.

After swimming, diving for objects and playing some pool volleyball, Brandon and his family lazed by the pool and chatted. Brandon learned that even though *Gōnggong* (公公) and *Pópo* (婆婆) now live in Beijing—*Běijīng* (北京), *Gōnggong* (公公) actually grew up in Hong Kong—*Xiānggǎng* (香港).

"Brandon, did you know that the local Hong Kongers speak a Chinese dialect called Cantonese[2] or *Guǎngdōng huà* (广东话)?" asked *Gōnggong* (公公).

"Huh? Dialect? What's that?" asked a befuddled Brandon.

"A dialect is a form of language that people speak in a specific part of a country. Let me teach you how to say hello in Cantonese," said *Gōnggong* (公公).

"There are a few different ways. Instead of '*nǐ hǎo* (你好)' like we say in Mandarin, it's '*néih hóu* (你好)' in Cantonese. However, that's a more formal greeting. Most people simply say '*Wèi* (喂)' or '*Hā luō* (哈囉)'."

---

[2] If you would like more information about Cantonese, please check out: www.eugeniachu.com/cantonese/

Brandon Goes to Hong Kong (Xiānggǎng 香港)

"Oh, let me try! *Néih hóu* (你好)! *Wèi* (喂)! *Hā luō* (哈囉)!"

"*Tài bàng le* (太棒了)—Awesome!" praised *Gōnggong* (公公). "But you don't have to say all three—just pick one!"

As Brandon laughed, a picture of a big red Chinese dragon appeared on the projector by the pool. *Gōnggong* (公公) turned to see what Brandon was looking at.

"Brandon, the Chinese dragon, or *lóng* (龙), is a symbol of the Chinese people. You will see it everywhere." *Gōnggong* (公公) proceeded to stand up and waved his hand to show off the little dragon decal that was sewn on the edge of his bathing suit. Everyone laughed!

Gōnggong (公公) then raised his arm toward the glass wall, "Even the kites flying outside are shaped like *lóng* (龙)."

Brandon looked, and then looked again. "One of the kites just winked at me!"

Gōnggong (公公) squinted in the light. "I just see regular kites. Nothing winking."

"Must have been the sun glinting off one of the kites," said Mom.

Brandon nodded. "Yeah, must have been."

Could one of the kites really have winked at Brandon? Were they all really just kites?

CHAPTER 3

Meeting Kelsey

That night at dinner, Brandon got to meet his second cousin[3], Kelsey. Kelsey was 7 ½ years old and attended an international school where most of her classes were taught in English—*Yīngwén* (英文).

---

[3] The naming of cousins can be very confusing! People who have the same grandparents are first cousins. People who have the same great-grandparents are second cousins. Brandon and Kelsey are second cousins because Kelsey's grandpa and *Gōnggong* (公公) are brothers, so Brandon and Kelsey have the same great-grandparents! In Chinese, there are even more names for differing levels of cousins depending on which side of the family they are on. Talk about confusing!

Brandon crossed his fingers. "I hope Kelsey's English is better than my Chinese!"

The restaurant where they were meeting was fancy, with lots of ornate wood carvings. They were having an early dinner so the restaurant was fairly empty and Brandon could tell immediately where Kelsey, her parents, and a few other aunties and uncles, were sitting. Kelsey wore a pink dress and sat quietly between her dad and mom.

"She looks nervous," thought Brandon as he glanced down at his hands, a bit anxious himself.

When Brandon's relatives saw them, all the adults jumped up and started shouting greetings and hugging them. This was a big reunion and everyone was excited to see one another and to meet Brandon. "It's a good thing the restaurant is empty," chuckled Brandon, "We are so loud!"

Once everyone was finally seated at the table, Brandon smiled at Kelsey and said quietly, "*Nǐ hǎo* (你好), Kelsey—I mean, *Hā luō* (哈囉)."

"Hello, Brandon *gēge* (哥哥)," whispered Kelsey barely looking up.

Brandon knew that *gēge* (哥哥) meant "big brother" and his heart melted a little. Brandon was an only child so he liked the idea of being a big brother to someone.

"Your English is very good, Kelsey. Do you like school?

Brandon Goes to Hong Kong (Xiānggǎng 香港)

Do you like learning English?"

"Thank you! Yes! I love school and I love English!" shouted Kelsey, no longer shy as she was talking about something she adored.

"What else do you like?" inquired Brandon.

"Princesses!" yelled Kelsey without any hesitation. "You should go to our Disneyland to see them! I have pictures with all of them. My favorite is Cinderella!"

Brandon nodded. He was not interested in princesses, but he wanted to be a good *gēge* (哥哥), so he went along with it. He did like the idea of going to Hong Kong Disneyland, though.

"Oh, and dragons! I love *lóng* (龙)!"

Before Brandon had a chance to comment about dragons, he smelled something so rich and fragrant it made his mouth water. A waiter brought out the most delicious-looking roast goose Brandon had ever seen or smelled. There were lots of oohs and ahs and *āiyōs* (哎哟).

Gōnggong (公公) was beaming! This just happened to be *Gōnggong*'s (公公) favorite dish at his favorite restaurant in all of *Xiānggǎng* (香港)! And the goose was perfectly cooked, tender and juicy covered with a crispy golden skin. Yum!

Brandon and Kelsey continued talking and getting to

know each other throughout their meal. They talked about school, their friends, favorite food and compared what it was like living in Miami versus Hong Kong. Occasionally, they needed a little help from their parents with translations, but overall, they had no trouble communicating with each other. Brandon was relieved!

Do you speak another language?

Brandon Goes to Hong Kong (Xiānggǎng 香港)

CHAPTER 4

Lantau Island and the Big Buddha

(Sunday)

The next morning, Brandon and his family went to a bustling, noisy dim sum restaurant for breakfast. Dim sum, or *diǎnxīn* (点心), are small bite-sized portions of food served in small steamer baskets or on small plates. There were so many yummy things to choose from. Lots and lots of workers were pushing carts filled with different types of delectable dishes—ranging from all kinds of dumplings, buns, fried delights, steamed vegetables, meats, desserts and everything in between. All you had to do was point at what you wanted from the cart when it came to your table and you got it!

"This is kind of like a buffet, except the tables come to you!" announced Brandon gleefully, as he took a big bite into what he called a "football"—a fried dumpling filled with aromatic meat in the shape of a football.

Brandon's favorite, however, was the Chinese dumplings, or *jiǎozi* (饺子). "These aren't as good as yours though, *Pópo* (婆婆)," mumbled Brandon over a mouthful of *jiǎozi* (饺子). "Will we be able to make any on this trip?" *Pópo* (婆婆) and Brandon had a special tradition of making *jiǎozi* (饺子) together whenever they could. It was one of Brandon's favorite things to do with *Pópo* (婆婆) and he always looked forward to it.

"We have a packed itinerary for this trip and we don't

Brandon Goes to Hong Kong (Xiānggǎng 香港)

have a kitchen here to make them, but I promise we will make *jiǎozi* (饺子) the next time we come visit you," assured *Pópo* (婆婆). Brandon's mouth was full so he gave her a big thumbs up, which made *Pópo* (婆婆) giggle. As the meal was winding down, Brandon patted his tummy and asked, "So where to now?"

Gōnggong (公公) answered, "Let's go to Lantau Island to see some Buddhist temples, a giant Buddha, called the Big Buddha or Tian Tan, and a small traditional village. We can travel there by a glass-bottom cable car!"

Giant Buddha? Glass bottom cable car? Brandon was sold. He nodded enthusiastically while shoving the last *jiǎozi* (饺子) into his mouth.

Riding the Ngong Ping 360 cable car with the glass bottom to the Big Buddha and Po Lin Monastery was like flying over the water and up the mountain.

As they were gliding over the water, *Gōnggong* (公公) pointed and said, "Look, Brandon, that is the Hong Kong-Zhuhai bridge. It's the world's longest sea bridge and is more than 34 miles! It was just finished in 2018, so it's a pretty new bridge. It connects Hong Kong to the Chinese mainland."

"That's super long!" exclaimed Brandon as he examined the long bridge snaking across the beautiful, shimmering blue-green water. "So, now you can drive from Hong Kong to China!"

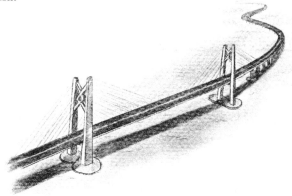

"You can if you have a special permit. But *Pópo* (婆婆) and I prefer to take the ferry. That way we can relax and enjoy the scenery while we travel. We prefer not to drive if we don't have to."

Below them, some people were flying kites shaped like dragons, or *lóng* (龙). One of the kites flipped its tail, flapped it wings, and turned into the sunlight. When its eyes met Brandon's, it suddenly disappeared!

"But, that can't be," argued Brandon to himself. When he looked again, they were too high up to see the flying dragon kites. "That was a real, live dragon!" Brandon murmured as he shook his head. "Or maybe the sun got in my eyes? Or something reflected off the glass of the cable car?"

Brandon Goes to Hong Kong (Xiānggǎng 香港)

Everybody was getting off the cable car at Ngong Ping Village when a little boy behind Brandon asked, "Did you see the dragon?"

The boy and his mother had just stepped into a car. Brandon scratched his head.

"Hmmm, I wonder..." he thought.

It was a gorgeous sunny day and Brandon and his family walked around the quaint little village with its cute stores and touristy restaurants, then headed to see the Big Buddha at the top of a very, very large hill.

"Yikes!" Brandon looked up at the majestic, giant, bronze Buddha in awe. "That's really big and really far up," cried Brandon, dreading having to climb all those stairs.

"Yes," said *Gōnggong* (公公), "it's almost 270 steps to the top. Let's see who can get up there first! But, no running and no bumping into people!"

Brandon, who loved a challenge, forgot about his initial apprehension and started up the steps with arms and legs pumping. "First!" Brandon shouted at the top. "We did it, *Gōnggong* (公公)!"

The view of Lantau Island was breathtaking. Brandon marveled at the sweeping mountain and sea views and smell of lush trees. And there were so many Buddhist statues all over—too many to count!

Admiring the statues, Brandon asked, "*Gōnggong* (公公), I know Buddhism is a religion, but I don't really understand it. "What are the teachings of Buddhism?"

"Buddhism teaches that people can end their own suffering by cutting out hatred, greed and ignorance. When people do bad things, bad things will happen to them. When people do good things, good things will happen to them."

"Like karma?" asked Brandon.

"Exactly—karma is a key belief in Buddhism," confirmed *Gōnggong* (公公).

"I like that, but why so many different Buddhas? Why do they all look different?"

Pópo (婆婆) responded, "The original historical Buddha was a man named Siddhartha Gautama, but 'Buddha' does not mean just one man who lived at a certain time. 'Buddha' is a person who has become enlightened, meaning they can see the true way the world works. There have been lots of Buddhas since Siddhartha Gautama."

"So Buddhas are not gods?" asked Brandon.

"Buddhas are teachers and are not considered gods. In fact, Buddhists in general don't believe in a god. But the Chinese Buddhists often pray to the various Buddhas for help and salvation, so some may consider them like gods," answered *Pópo* (婆婆).

Brandon Goes to Hong Kong (Xiānggǎng 香港)

"You know, Brandon," said Mom, "let's take some time later and research more. Understanding different beliefs is so important and I would like to learn more about Buddhism myself."

Brandon agreed, "Good idea! It'll be fun to research together when we get home."

As the family walked back down the hill, Brandon thought about the dragon kite that looked like a real live *lóng* (龙), and the comment by the little boy. He didn't say anything since he was sure it was just a figment of his imagination. The little boy could have been talking about anything—maybe he saw a dragon kite or a drawing of a dragon somewhere. But how amazing would it be if Brandon and the boy had both seen a real *lóng* (龙)! Too bad Kelsey was in school, because Brandon wanted to ask her about the *lóng* (龙). Since she was from Hong Kong and loves dragons, she wouldn't think he was crazy.

What do you think Brandon saw? Was it real or just his imagination?

CHAPTER 5

Victoria Peak

(Monday)

The next day, Brandon and his parents and grandparents went to visit one of Hong Kong's most popular attractions, Victoria Peak, the most famous and highest hill on Hong Kong Island. They took the Peak Tram and rode up the side of the mountain almost to the top of the Peak.

"Brandon," called *Gōnggong* (公公) as he waved Brandon over. "Look out over there."

Brandon Goes to Hong Kong (Xiānggǎng 香港)

Brandon was treated to the most picturesque view of *Xiānggǎng* (香港). He had views of the whole city and its waterfront on the South China Sea. Brandon was in awe of how beautiful *Xiānggǎng* (香港) was and amazed by how far he could see. It was a fabulous day and Brandon was enjoying the warm sun on his face and the cool breeze from the ocean. To Brandon's dismay, his parents started taking a GAZILLION pictures and made him pose for ALL of them. Brandon hated being in pictures and grunted, but he put on his best fake smile for every picture to make his parents happy.

"I hope they appreciate this," grumbled Brandon as he forced another fake smile.

"Thank you—*Xiè xiè* (谢谢)," said Mom. "I know you dislike taking pictures and we appreciate your cooperation. Who knows when we will be able to come back here? These photos will help us remember our trip. We can get some ice cream—*bīngqílín* (冰淇淋) afterwards." This made Brandon a little happier.

"Brandon, look at how great some of these pictures came out!" exclaimed Mom. She scrolled through the photos on her phone. Something red was flying in the background of one of the pictures.

Brandon burst out, "Go back to the last picture, Mom!" Brandon looked at the picture again, but the object in the background was unclear. He looked out over the horizon, but nothing was there. No red flying object as far as the eye could see.

"Mom, what do you think that red thing is in the picture? What is that—*Nà shì shénme* (那是什么)?" asked Brandon pointing to the red thing.

"I'm not sure," said Mom squinting. "It could be anything—maybe a balloon or kite that flew away, or maybe it's just a piece of fuzz that floated in front of the camera."

What do you think that red object in the picture was? Could it possibly be a red dragon kite? Could it be more?

CHAPTER 6

Victoria Harbour Symphony of Lights

That evening, Brandon was still thinking about the red blur in the picture while he was getting ready for dinner. "Hurry up, Brandon, everyone is waiting for us upstairs!" called Mom.

Brandon shook his head to clear his mind and quickly finished getting dressed. They were meeting everyone at the restaurant at the top of their hotel for dinner and to watch the Symphony of Lights show over Victoria Harbour.

When Brandon and his parents got to the restaurant, *Gōnggong* (公公), *Pópo* (婆婆), Kelsey and several aunts and uncles were already seated at a big table facing the harbor. They were really high up! Brandon slid in next to Kelsey and said, "*Hā luō* (哈囉) Kesley! How was school today?"

"Great!" replied Kelsey, and proceeded to describe in great detail everything she had done at school that day—starting with how her dad had dropped her off in the morning with a silly dance and ending with how her mom had picked her up in the afternoon with a big hug. She showed Brandon a small red paper dragon she had made at school.

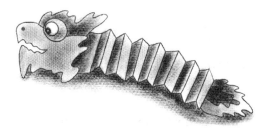

"Whoa!" uttered Brandon. "This is too much of a coincidence! I have to ask you someth..."

Before Brandon could finish his sentence, music played and lights flashed. *Gōnggong* (公公) bellowed, "It's starting—*Kāishile* (开始了)!"

Gōnggong (公公) explained, "This show is the world's

largest permanent light and sound show, and starts every night at 8:00 p.m. The colored lasers and lights shoot from the top of 40 buildings lining the Hong Kong skyline, including from this hotel." He pointed up and continued, "The music is a recording by the Hong Kong Philharmonic Orchestra. Not bad, right?"

Everyone watched the light show, which was truly spectacular! The whole harbor was set ablaze as thousands of lasers, searchlights, LED screens and lighting all worked together to create a transformational feast for the eyes and ears!

"This never gets old," sighed one of Brandon's aunties, while everyone else nodded in agreement.

Once the show was over, everyone continued chatting and eating dinner. Kelsey, with a mouth full of noodles, turned to Brandon and mumbled, "Hey, Brandon *gēge* (哥哥), what were you saying before?"

Brandon looked down at the paper dragon sitting next to Kelsey on her seat and asked, "Where did you get the idea to make a red dragon—*lóng* (龙)?" He really wanted to ask if *lóng* (龙) were real, but didn't want to risk getting laughed at—*lóng* (龙) were just made-up creatures like fairies and goblins, right? He definitely didn't believe in those. He was much too grown up to believe in fairytales!

Kelsey replied, "Our teacher had us make something

we saw over the weekend. I saw a *lóng* (龙), so that's what I made."

"You *saw* a *lóng* (龙)?" asked Brandon incredulously. Brandon could feel his heart starting to beat fast and hard as he anticipated Kelsey's response.

"Yes, there were lots of people flying kites because the weather was so nice. I saw lots of dragon kites..." and then Kelsey looked down and paused, "and I saw something...else."

"What? What did you see? Tell me!" pleaded Brandon.

Kelsey looked at Brandon sheepishly and asked, "Promise you won't laugh or think I'm a silly little girl?"

"Of course I won't! I would never!" promised Brandon.

Kelsey took a deep breath and continued, "I think I saw a real *lóng* (龙) flying with the dragon kites. I looked really hard and I couldn't see any strings and it looked alive!"

"Did anyone else see it?" Brandon inquired, staring at Kelsey with wide eyes.

"No," whispered Kelsey, "when I turned to find my parents to show them, it disappeared. When I told them what I saw they said it must have been one of the kites."

"I think I saw the same thing when we were in the cable car going up to see the Big Buddha! I couldn't get a good look so I figured it was my imagination. Then at Victoria's

Brandon Goes to Hong Kong (Xiānggǎng 香港)

Peak, something red in the sky showed up in one of the pictures—but it wasn't clear. Let me show you." Brandon borrowed Mom's phone to show Kelsey.

Kelsey looked hard turning the phone this way and that. She finally said, "Yeah, it's too hard to tell."

"But, maybe there really is a real *lóng* (龙) flying around *Xiānggǎng* (香港)—how awesome would that be!" smiled Brandon.

"That would be so, so, so GREAT!" Kelsey nodded happily and gave Brandon the biggest smile of the night.

"How about this—I'll ask around and do some research on dragons to see what I can find out about them. Why don't you ask your teacher at school tomorrow what she knows about dragons and we can talk more the next time we meet?" suggested Brandon.

And just like that, Brandon and Kelsey had a plan.

What do you think Brandon and Kelsey will discover through their research? Will they ever see a real lóng (龙)?

CHAPTER 7

Researching Dragons: Part 1

When Brandon and his family got back to their room that night, Brandon got ready for bed, said goodnight to his parents, and then went straight to his computer to research dragons. He learned there were lots of different types of dragons. Some were scary and mean, some were cute and friendly and others were regal and brought good luck. It seemed that dragons looked and acted differently in various parts of the world.

"All of this research is only showing the pretend dragons in fairy tales and legends," murmured Brandon. "I need to find some information about real dragons."

As Brandon was typing in a new search, Mom walked in and said, "*Wa* (哇), Brandon, it's so late! I thought you were already asleep! We have a big day ahead of us. Go to sleep—*Qù shuìjiào* (去睡觉)."

Brandon quickly scrambled into bed as Mom smiled and tucked him in. As she leaned down to give him a kiss, Brandon whispered, "Are dragons real?"

"Komodo dragons are real. Maybe we will see one tomorrow. Goodnight—*Wǎn'ān* (晚安)," Mom whispered back as she turned off the lights and closed the door.

"I wonder what Komodo dragons are. I wonder if that is what I saw," pondered Brandon as he fell asleep and dreamt of flying red dragons.

Do you think Brandon will really see a dragon tomorrow?

CHAPTER 8

Ocean Park

(Tuesday)

The next morning, Brandon heard a tap-tap-tap on his door. He was still dreaming about a big red dragon and when he opened his eyes, he expected to see one! However, it was just Dad smiling at the door. "Wake up, Brandon. Today we are going to Ocean Park!"

"What's Ocean Park?" groaned Brandon while rubbing the sleep from his eyes.

"Ocean Park is Hong Kong's largest theme park—even bigger than Disneyland! Actually, it's more than just a theme park—it's a zoo, a marine animal park and an amusement park all in one! And..." Dad paused.

"And what?!?!" asked Brandon. In his excitement he momentarily forgot all about his dragon dream.

"And...*Gōnggong* (公公) signed us all up for the Honorary Panda Keeper Program where we will be able to see the pandas up close! *Gōnggong* (公公) will tell you all about it during breakfast."

Brandon excitedly hopped out of bed. He loved pandas, called *xióng māo* (熊猫) in Chinese. He and his cousins from California became friends with a very special *xióng māo* (熊猫), named *Xiǎo Míng* (小明), when they were in *Běijīng* (北京) the previous year. *Gōnggong* (公公) and *Pópo* (婆婆), who live in *Běijīng* (北京), started going to the Beijing Zoo every week to visit *Xiǎo Míng* (小明). They would send videos and pictures to Brandon. Brandon would also send messages to *Xiǎo Míng* (小明) that *Gōnggong* (公公) and *Pópo* (婆婆) would pass on.

Brandon and his parents met *Gōnggong* (公公) and *Pópo* (婆婆) for a traditional Hong Kong breakfast of rice porridge, called congee, and fried dough sticks, called *yóutiáo* (油条). Brandon loved the crispy, greasy *yóutiáo* (油条).

"How come we never have *yóutiáo* (油条) for breakfast at home?" Brandon asked Mom.

"Because they are not healthy for you…and I don't know how to make them," confessed Mom. Everyone laughed.

While they ate, *Gōnggong* (公公) told them about the fun rides at Ocean Park and then explained the Honorary Panda Keeper Program.

"Through the Honorary Panda Keeper Program, we will see first hand how to take care of pandas—*xióng māo* (熊猫). We will learn how to prepare their toys and meals and help the keepers clean up. We will learn all about *xióng māo* (熊猫) and their habitat and what we can do to help keep them safe."

"Wow! I wonder if any of them will be able to talk like *Xiǎo Míng* (小明)," wondered Brandon out loud.

"I doubt it," said *Pópo* (婆婆). "*Xiǎo Míng* (小明) is a very rare breed of *xióng māo* (熊猫), maybe the last of his kind."

"Yeah, I know," frowned Brandon. But then he perked up and smiled as he said, "That's okay, I love all pandas and am super excited to see any *xióng māo* (熊猫)! We don't have any by us at home. They are so cute—*hǎo kě ài* (好可爱)! I can't wait!"

Ocean Park was divided into two parts—a lower level and an upper level.

"Let's start at the upper level. You can travel from one level to the other either by a sky tram or a submarine-themed train that goes through the mountain," explained *Gōnggong* (公公). "Which would you like to take first?"

"Let's take the sky tram," suggested Brandon, "then we can take the train to come back."

The sky tram provided a stunning and unhindered view of the sea, sky and surrounding hills along with lots of the rides at the Park. It reminded Brandon of the Ngong Ping 360 cable car they took to see the Big Buddha—where he first thought he saw a *lóng* (龙). Brandon shook his head to clear his mind and focused on the view.

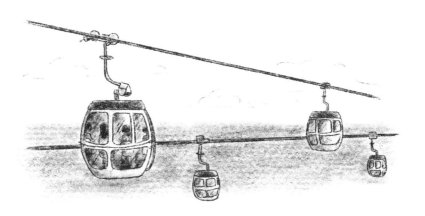

At the upper level, called the Summit, Brandon rode a ton of fun rides, tossed fish to the sea lions, watched seals getting their teeth brushed, saw other beautiful animals from around the world and enjoyed some interactive shows.

On the way back to the lower level, Brandon and his family took the submarine-themed train through a fantastical underwater journey to the Waterfront where there was a huge aquarium, a playground for younger kids and the pandas—*xióng māo* (熊猫).

"It's time to join the Honorary Panda Keeper Program!" announced *Gōnggong* (公公). Brandon and his family all got special uniforms to wear, and then went behind the scenes of the panda enclosure to help with the *xióng māo* (熊猫). It was a lot of work but lots of fun, too! The panda keepers told them a bunch of funny stories about their jobs taking care of the *xióng māo* (熊猫). Brandon's favorite thing was feeding the *xióng māo* (熊猫). Brandon talked to them, but none of them replied or even appeared to understand him.

"Guess these pandas are not related to *Xiǎo Míng* (小明)," decided Brandon sadly, as he fed them the bamboo he had personally chosen for them. They were beautiful and amazing. Brandon loved how they gently took the bamboo from his hand and slowly munched on it. He smiled. "I'm so lucky to be here," he said with a sigh. "This is the highlight of my day."

The smallest *xióng māo* (熊猫) cub looked right at Brandon and pointed up. Brandon looked to where the tiny *xióng māo* (熊猫) was pointing. A red object flew overhead!

"Hey! Do you guys see that? What is that—*Nà shì shénme* (那是什么)?"

Everyone looked at Brandon, but the red figure was gone. "Did anyone see something red flying in the sky?" No one responded for what seemed like forever.

"Maybe you saw a balloon," suggested one of the panda keepers. "Sometimes kids accidently let go of their balloons and they end up flying away. It's actually very bad for the environment—we are trying to discourage people from using balloons."

Brandon looked at the baby *xióng māo* (熊猫), but she was busy eating bamboo and wouldn't look back at him.

"How strange," uttered Brandon under his breath.

Did the panda cub really point at something in the sky? Or is Brandon's imagination working overtime?

Brandon Goes to Hong Kong (Xiānggǎng 香港)

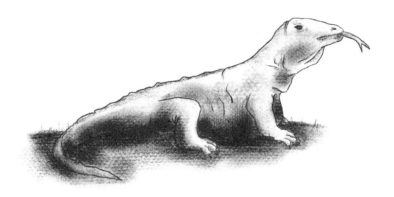

CHAPTER 9

Real Live Dragons

Brandon and his family changed back to their own clothes and were leaving the panda exhibit. Brandon mentioned, "Mom, I thought you said we might see a dragon today."

Mom responded, "Oh yes! I read that there is a visiting Komodo Dragon Exhibit here now. Let's go check it out." Brandon started to do his happy dance!

They crossed the bridge over the fish pond to the dragon exhibit. Mom pointed. "Look at that Komodo dragon—it's huge!"

Brandon didn't see any big red dragons. "Where?" he asked, "I don't see any dragons."

"Right here," said Mom as she walked toward a giant brown lizard creature sitting on a rock. "Isn't he majestic? Komodo dragons are from Indonesia and are the world's largest lizards."

Brandon thought the Komodo dragon was cool, but he was a bit disappointed. It wasn't what he was expecting and looked nothing like the winged creature he thought he had previously seen. It was a big, brown lizard, but it was smaller than what he'd seen. And it didn't have wings. There was no way this thing could fly!

"Are there bigger Komodo dragons? Are any of them red? Can any of them fly?" Brandon questioned in rapid succession.

Mr. Tam, the Komodo dragon exhibit keeper, was standing nearby and overheard Brandon's queries.

"What great questions, young man!" said Mr. Tam. "Komodos typically grow to around 6–9 feet and weigh up to 200 pounds, but the largest one we know of is 10.3 feet and weighs 366 pounds! Komodos come in a variety of colors, including blue, orange, green and gray—but not red, at least not that I've seen. Komodos are also venomous—so make sure you don't get too close to one in case it bites you!"

Brandon Goes to Hong Kong (Xiānggǎng 香港)

"Wow! Komodos are cool! But, are there any other dragons that you know of? Any that can maybe fly? And are red?" asked Brandon.

"Well, the Draco is called the Flying Dragon. It can glide half the length of a football field! Loose folds of skin on its sides stretch to form a cape, enabling it to 'fly.' These 'wings' are a bit translucent so they can look red, but their bodies are more tan or brown and a bit spotty. They are much smaller than the Komodos. We don't have any here but I can show you a picture, if you like."

Brandon and his family followed Mr. Tam to his office where he showed them a few pictures of the Flying Dragon. They were very cute and had red wings, which were really just flaps of skin, but this was not the dragon Brandon was hoping to see.

"Thanks so much for showing me the Flying Dragon," said Brandon.

A drawing of a red dragon with a long body, big wings and four legs on a calendar hung on the wall by the door.

"What's that?" asked Brandon pointing to the dragon on the calendar.

"Oh, that's my dragon calendar. Each month has a drawing of a different mythical dragon. This is the typical Chinese dragon, or *lóng* (龙). Most dragon kites and dragons used in parades are modeled after it. Beautiful, isn't it?" Brandon agreed, thinking that this was the dragon he saw—or maybe imagined seeing.

Mr. Tam proceeded to show Brandon the other mythical dragons in his calendar: Quetzalcoatl, Western dragon, Hydra, Dragonnet and Wyvern.

Mr. Tam explained that the Chinese dragon and the Western dragon, while very different, are the most common dragons depicted in movies, books and legends.

"Wow! I didn't know there were so many different types of dragons. It's all so interesting!" asserted Brandon.

"Yes, I love all dragons! If you ever want to talk about dragons, either mythical or real, you know where to find me. Thanks for coming by," called Mr. Tam as he waved goodbye to Brandon and his family.

Based on the information from Mr. Tam and his own initial research, Brandon knew he needed to focus his search on Chinese dragons. The dragon he saw—or thought he saw—did not look like a Western dragon or any of the other dragons. And it definitely wasn't a Komodo dragon or a Draco.

As they were leaving Ocean Park, Brandon asked, "*Gōnggong* (公公), *Pópo* (婆婆)—what do you know about Chinese dragons—*lóng* (龙)?

Brandon Goes to Hong Kong (Xiānggǎng 香港)

Chinese dragon—*lóng* (龙)

Quetzalcoatl

Western dragon

Hydra

Dragonnet

Wyvern

"Well, *lóng* (龙) are legendary creatures in Chinese mythology and folklore. They date back to, and maybe even before, the first Chinese dynasty, the Xia Dynasty, in 2100 BC. That's over 4000 years ago! *Lóng* (龙) became the symbol of the Emperor because of its strength and power. Stories about them have been told through the ages. They are symbols of luck and power for the Chinese," explained *Pópo* (婆婆), who used to teach Chinese history.

Brandon saw an ice cream shop coming up and pointed. "Ice cream—*bīngqílín* (冰淇淋)!"

As Brandon licked his vanilla ice cream, or *bīngqílín* (冰淇淋), he asked, "what color is the Chinese *lóng* (龙)? Is it scary?"

Pópo (婆婆) paused between licks of her *bīngqílín* (冰淇淋).

"There are several different types of legendary or mythical *lóng* (龙) and they come in different colors, but the most popular one is the red one you saw on the calendar in Mr. Tam's office. *Lóng* (龙) aren't seen as monsters as portrayed in the West."

"Aren't lots of legends based on true things? Could *lóng* (龙) be real?" asked Brandon, holding his breath.

"Some are stories passed down through the ages that

include an element of truth, but I think *lóng* (龙) is a mythical creature that is more symbolic than real," responded *Pópo* (婆婆).

"I don't know, I think *lóng* (龙) might be real," winked *Gōnggong* (公公).

"Don't tease him," *Pópo* (婆婆) laughed as she playfully hit *Gōnggong* (公公) on the shoulder. *Gōnggong* (公公) just shrugged and smiled.

Could *lóng* (龙) be real? Does *Gōnggong* (公公) know something or is he just kidding around?

CHAPTER 10

Dinner with Kelsey

That evening, Brandon was having dinner with Kelsey and the rest of the family. As soon as Kelsey saw Brandon, she ran over. Before even saying hello, she blurted, "My teacher says her favorite stories are about dragons, but that they are made up—they're not real." Kelsey's bottom lip quivered as her eyes started to water.

"Hi Kelsey! *Wèi* (喂)! Don't be upset. There are Komodo dragons and Dracos, which are called Flying Dragons, but they are really just very cool lizards," explained a now quite educated Brandon. "No one seems to believe that the *lóng* (龙) that we are thinking of is real, except for maybe *Gōnggong* (公公), but I'm going to do a little more digging."

During dinner Brandon filled everyone in on his adventures at Ocean Park, spending most of the time describing the Honorary Panda Keeper Program and explaining all that he learned about dragons and lizards. Everyone was quite impressed! After much discussion, everyone, except for *Gōnggong* (公公) and Kelsey, was of the opinion that *lóng* (龙) are not real.

The topic then switched to Disneyland, where Brandon was going the next day. Kelsey started dancing on her seat.

"Brandon *gēge* (哥哥), promise me that you will visit at least one princess and tell her that I say hello. Please!" Kelsey appeared to have forgotten their quest for the almighty and magical *lóng* (龙), which was clearly overshadowed by princesses!

Will Brandon continue his research on dragons? What does *Gōnggong* (公公) know?

CHAPTER 11

Hong Kong Disneyland

(Wednesday)

The next morning, Brandon woke up bright and early and rushed to get ready for Disneyland. Disneyland Hong Kong was split into different "lands" with each following a unique theme. Most of the main rides were similar to those at home, although the stories and songs—like on the "It's a Small World" ride—along with the instructions around the park, were in English AND Cantonese AND Mandarin.

"Cool!" remarked Brandon. "How international!"

Brandon Goes to Hong Kong (Xiānggǎng 香港)

To his delight, the lines were much shorter than at the Disney World at home. The main difference was the food.

"The food here is much yummier and there are lots more options!" declared a delighted Brandon while doing his happy dance.

As the family was getting ready to leave after a fun, but long, day, Brandon remembered his promise to Kelsey. He saw a line to meet characters, so he grimaced and joined the other parkgoers, mostly young girls, waiting to take a picture with a Disney princess.

"I hope this is worth it. I'm such a good *gēge* (哥哥)—big brother," Brandon said as he patted himself on the back.

When it was Brandon's turn to meet the princess, someone dressed in a dragon costume strutted by. "Hey, I know you from a movie!" The dragon nodded and high-fived Brandon.

"Will you take a picture with me and the princess?" The dragon nodded again and followed Brandon.

"Hi, my name is Brandon. My cousin Kelsey says hello. She's a big fan."

"That's so nice! Be sure to give Kelsey a big hug from me," smiled the princess.

"Do you know what kind of dragon this is?" Brandon pointed at the dragon character standing next to him.

"He's a very special Chinese dragon and my personal guardian," answered the princess.

"Do you think there are real dragons?" grilled Brandon.

"They are real if you believe they are real," sang the princess.

"Okay, that's a very princess thing to say, I suppose," Brandon thought as he smiled politely at the princess.

After Brandon got his picture taken with the princess and the dragon, he went to the store and bought a little stuffed dragon, along with a package containing all the Disney princesses for Kelsey.

"Kelsey is going to be so surprised," Brandon said as Dad was paying for the gifts.

On the way back to the hotel, Brandon started thinking about the dragon character he met and how he resembled the dragon he saw, or thought he saw.

"Maybe that's why I thought I saw what I saw…I just watched the movie with that very princess and dragon the other week!"

Are dragons real? Will Brandon ever find out?

CHAPTER 12

Researching Dragons: Part 2

By the time Brandon got back to the hotel, he still had some time before he had to go to bed. He decided to do some more research. First, he searched for "real dragons" on the internet. He found Komodo and flying dragons (which he now knew all about), dragonsnakes (which looked like snakes), bearded dragons (which one of his friends has as a very cute pet named Gidget), and various fish and bugs that had the word "dragon" in their name. None of these matched what he saw—or thought he saw. So, he continued to search.

Gidget the Bearded Dragon

Brandon looked for lizards that look like dragons—because maybe what he saw was really just a big, flying, red lizard. He saw pictures of the Chinese Water Dragon, Plumed Basilisk, Crested Gecko and Red-Eyed Crocodile Skinks. These lizards did resemble little dragons, but looked nothing like the dragon Brandon thought he saw.

Brandon sighed as his shoulders slumped. "Maybe I just imagined a dragon based on the stories I've heard, movies I've watched and the dragon kites and dragon dances I've seen."

Brandon tapped his temple. "Let me check one more thing. Everyone says dragons are mythical or legendary creatures…" He then began a new search on whether legends are ever based on truth. "If the legend of the *lóng* (龙) is based on truth, maybe *lóng* (龙) are real. Maybe they are hiding and maybe people don't see them because they don't believe they exist."

Brandon got to work. A legend is a traditional story sometimes regarded as historical but unauthenticated; and a myth is also a traditional story, but one concerning the early history of people and typically involving supernatural beings or events.

"Okay," breathed Brandon, "nothing here says that legend and myths are always fake—just that they are unproven. I wonder if any mythical or legendary creatures have ever turned out to be real?"

Brandon got excited—he found that there really were such creatures. The narwhal, platypus, rhinoceros and giant squid were all believed to be mythological or legendary creatures before they were proven to be real.

"Wow! People thought these animals were all imagined, but now we know they actually exist! They do sound totally made up if you were to describe them," chuckled Brandon.

When Mom and Dad walked in to check on Brandon, he asked them, "Hey, what would you say if I told you there was a creature with the feet of an elephant, the tail of a boar and a single horn on its head? Would you think that was a real animal or a mythical creature?"

"Mythical," answered Mom and Dad in unison.

"Nope! It's a rhino!" declared Brandon. "Long ago people thought rhinos were mythical, just like people today think *lóng* (龙) are fake. And just like they thought narwhals were mythical until fairly recently. So maybe there's a possibility that *lóng* (龙) are real but just haven't been proven yet. What do you think?"

Mom and Dad were impressed with Brandon's research and logic, but they grew up believing the stories about *lóng* (龙) were just that—stories. But, Brandon had made a good argument, so Dad said, "It's unlikely, but maybe there could be some reality behind the myth."

"Maybe," concurred Mom, "but it's bedtime—*shuìjiào shíjiān* (睡觉时间), so go wash up."

"Aw, Mom, can I stay up a little longer to do some more research?" pleaded Brandon.

"How about you sleep on what you've learned tonight and continue your research in the morning? We can order breakfast from room service and head out a little later. Sound good?"

"Yes!" Brandon jumped up to brush his teeth. Brandon loved getting room service and eating breakfast in his pajamas!

That night Brandon dreamt of narwhals and platypuses and rhinos—oh my! And he dreamt they were all playing with a flying red *lóng* (龙)!

Could dragons be real like narwhals, platypuses and rhinoceroses?

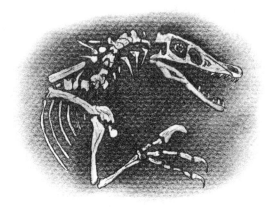

CHAPTER 13

Researching Dragons: Part 3
(Thursday)

The next morning, Brandon searched the news for instances where people may have seen or found dragons. A few articles reported that people may have discovered dinosaur fossils believing they were the remains of dragons. He found documentation that at least one historian from China had labeled such a fossil as a dragon back in the 4th century B.C.

"Well, just because some people in the past confused dragons with dinosaurs doesn't disprove that dragons exist," scowled Brandon as he munched on a piece of bacon, his favorite breakfast food ever.

Brandon also found a few articles reporting that a village in northern China thought they discovered the skeleton of a dead dragon a few years ago, but it was never confirmed and many thought it might have been a hoax or set up for a movie or something. Brandon didn't find anything conclusive by the time they were leaving the hotel.

Will Brandon learn anything to confirm that dragons could be real?

CHAPTER 14

Star Ferry and Kowloon; Mid-Levels Escalator

After breakfast, Brandon and his parents, along with *Gōnggong* (公公) and *Pópo* (婆婆), walked down to Victoria Harbour and boarded the iconic Hong Kong Star Ferry.

"Hey, I've seen this ferry boat in almost every picture and postcard of Hong Kong—*Xiānggǎng* (香港)!" proclaimed Brandon.

"Yes, the Star Ferry has been operating for well over a century and is one of the city's oldest modes of transporta-

Brandon Goes to Hong Kong (Xiānggǎng 香港)

tion. It's famous—everyone knows it," confirmed *Gōnggong* (公公). "Tourists and locals alike take it. In fact, more than 50,000 passengers ride it every day! I think this is the most scenic and pleasant way to get to Kowloon. It's definitely my favorite way."

For the next 20 minutes, Brandon enjoyed the gorgeous views from the water and took lots of pictures to show his friends back home. When they arrived at Kowloon, a peninsula right across the harbor from Hong Kong Island, Brandon walked by lots of stores, parks and museums. But what Brandon liked the best was the views of Hong Kong Island.

"So many skyscrapers!" he exclaimed.

"Many people refer to *Xiānggǎng* (香港) as the 'concrete jungle'," added *Gōnggong* (公公).

"That totally makes sense—very descriptive," said Brandon.

The way back to the Hong Kong side was just as beautiful as the trip leaving it. From the ferry, Brandon spotted a dragon dance performance. Brandon turned to *Gōnggong* (公公) and pointed, "Look! I thought dragon dances were only for Chinese New Year!"

Gōnggong (公公) responded, "The dragon dance is mainly reserved for Chinese New Year, but it may also be performed at special celebrations like weddings and other

important occasions such as business openings. Sometimes it may be used to honor special foreign guests. That looks like a wedding celebration."

The dragon dancers were very skillful as they twisted and turned the dragon's body so elegantly in tune to the drumming. Brandon watched for as long as he could, but the ferry was taking them father and farther away until Brandon could only see a blur of color. There was a blur of red in the sky above the performance, too.

"Could it be?" considered Brandon wistfully. "Nah, I just have *lóng* (龙) on the brain."

When they were back, *Gōnggong* (公公) said, "Since it's still early, let me show you the largest outdoor covered escalator in the world, called the Mid-Levels Escalator. It's located in Central Hong Kong and it's about half a mile long!

Brandon Goes to Hong Kong (Xiānggǎng 香港)

It's a fun way to get around hilly Hong Kong."

"Wow," said Brandon, "that's way better than walking!"

The Mid-Levels Escalator was so long! And there were a bunch of entry and exit points, rest areas, and even cafes and shops. Brandon and his family had fun hopping on and off along the route to explore and stop for snacks.

"See how the escalator is going up now?" gestured *Gōnggong* (公公). Brandon nodded.

"In the mornings, the escalator runs downhill to take people to work, then switches directions at around 10:00 a.m. to run uphill until midnight, at which point it turns off until the morning."

When they were at the highest point of the escalator and started heading down, something red flashed overhead.

"What was that?" motioned Brandon. At that same exact moment, a girl about Brandon's age was also pointing up and shouting something in Cantonese—*Guǎngdōng huà* (广东话). But, nothing was there when everyone turned to look. Brandon just shook his head. The girl looked at Brandon and shrugged and walked off with her parents.

"I wonder…" mused Brandon.

Is Brandon seeing things? Did the girl see the same thing?

CHAPTER 15

Last Night in Xiānggǎng (香港)

That evening was Brandon and his parents' last evening in *Xiānggǎng* (香港) and the last time he would see Kelsey for a long time. Dinner was delicious but Kelsey hadn't smiled once.

Then Brandon remembered that he still had the stuffed dragon and princesses for Kelsey! "Kelsey, don't be sad. I almost forgot—I have a gift for you!"

Kelsey's eyes lit up. "What? What is it—*Shì shénme* (是什么)?"

Brandon Goes to Hong Kong (Xiānggǎng 香港)

Brandon smiled and handed her the dragon toy and package of princesses, and then he showed her the picture he had taken. "This princess says hi and sends you a hug."

"Really—*Zhēn de ma* (真的吗)?" squealed Kelsey as she hugged her stuffed dragon tight. "That's so cool! Thank you, Brandon *gēge* (哥哥), for doing all this for me! Thank you, thank you—*Xiè xiè* (谢谢), *xiè xiè* (谢谢)!"

Brandon was glad that he was able to make Kelsey so happy. "I guess it was worth standing in that line to meet a princess after all," smiled Brandon.

As Kelsey was playing with her dragon, she looked up at Brandon and asked, "Do you still think *lóng* (龙) might be real?"

"I don't know," responded Brandon. "There is no proof that *lóng* (龙) exist, but the Disney princess told me that if you believe, then they are real."

Kelsey nodded, "She would know!"

"It would be fun to believe in *lóng* (龙), don't you think?" asked Brandon.

"Yes, it would be fun. I would like to believe!" answered Kelsey.

"Me too," agreed Brandon. "Let's believe."

Kelsey clapped with glee and then made her dragon toy fly through the air.

While Brandon was taking a bite of rice, he thought he saw the toy's reflection in the window from the corner of his eye, but when he looked back at Kelsey, she was busy eating dinner. Brandon looked toward the window again, but there was nothing. "Hmmm..."

Will Brandon solve this mystery before leaving for home?

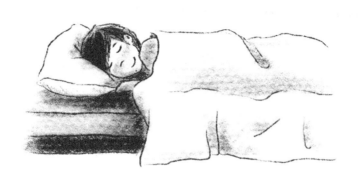

CHAPTER 16

The Dream?

Brandon was still thinking about *lóng* (龙), when he went to bed that night. The room was nice and cool and Brandon pulled the covers all the way up to his chin. He loved sleeping all bundled up and fell asleep almost instantly.

A strange sound woke Brandon. He looked out the glass door which led to the balcony off his room. Brandon couldn't believe his eyes! Was that a *lóng* (龙) out there?!?!

Brandon rubbed his eyes and looked again. It was still there! It was red and long and HUGE—and it was hovering by his balcony! "Whaaaat...?"

Brandon slowly tiptoed over to the door, trying not to make a sound, and put his hand on the door handle. He didn't want to make any sudden or loud noises which might scare away the great *lóng* (龙). He looked out and the flying red *lóng* (龙) was looking right at him! The dragon's eyes were big and kind. It looked friendly so Brandon opened the door and whispered, "Hi—*Hā luō* (哈囉)."

"Hi Brandon," breathed the *lóng* (龙).

"You can speak? And you know my name?" gasped Brandon. His eyes widened and goosebumps formed on his arms and legs.

"I know everyone's names and I know all languages—even Chinglish, a combination of English and Chinese!" snickered the giant, obviously humorous, *lóng* (龙). "I don't speak with my mouth and vocal chords like you do. I simply communicate through thoughts, so whatever language is most comfortable for you is the language we will use."

Brandon noticed that the *lóng* (龙) did not move its mouth and the sound of its words were in his head. "Wow! So, you mean like telepathy? That's so cool!"

The *lóng* (龙) nodded and added, "I can communicate with all creatures. My name is unpronounceable by humans, but you may call me Eon, since I have been around forever."

Brandon was stunned silent for a moment before quickly recovering and exclaiming, "Wow! That's incredible! I'm so honored to meet you, Eon!"

"The honor is all mine," bowed Eon. "Would you like to hop on my back and go for a ride? Let me show you how I see Hong Kong—*Xiānggǎng* (香港)."

Brandon whooped and immediately stepped from his balcony onto Eon's back. After all, he didn't want this majestic and astonishing creature to change his mind! Brandon settled onto Eon's back. His skin was soft and smooth, despite it looking hard and scaly. The beautiful red color reflected the light and sparkled. Eon's body was long like a snake, and he had horns on his head like a deer. Brandon was enthralled and enchanted with this magnificent creature!

Brandon held on as tight as he could as Eon spread his wings and took off in flight. At first, he squeezed his eyes closed and gripped tightly onto Eon's back. Eon felt Brandon's fear and told him, "Don't worry, Brandon, you won't fall off, even if you completely let go."

Brandon slowly opened his eyes and loosened his grip. He looked around and relaxed. He *was* safe and secure on Eon's back. He let go and threw his arms up above his head and yelled, "Woo hoo!" It was exhilarating!

Eon flew Brandon around the harbor and showed him all the bright lights of *Xiānggǎng* (香港). The wind whipped through Brandon's hair as they flew over Victoria Harbour and The Peak. The salty air filled his lungs. Everything looked so small, including the Star Ferry which was alit like a firefly. They flew over the Hong Kong-Zhuhai bridge, which shone like a giant sparkling snake. They passed by the Big Buddha, which still looked pretty big. They traveled all around Hong Kong Island. Brandon blinked at all the lights shining throughout this beautiful city. He had never imagined he would see *Xiānggǎng* (香港) like this. His heart was full of happiness!

As the first hint of the sun appeared over the horizon, Eon brought Brandon back to his room.

Brandon Goes to Hong Kong (Xiānggǎng 香港)

"Have a good sleep, Brandon. I had fun showing you my *Xiānggǎng* (香港) tonight. I hope you will remember this experience, and me, forever."

Before Brandon could respond, Eon was gone. "How did he disappear like that? I have so many questions..." yawned Brandon as he climbed back into bed. He was asleep by the time his head hit his pillow.

A loud knock on the door jolted Brandon from his sleep. He was a bit dazed and confused when Dad walked in and sang, "Time to get up, sleepyhead. Breakfast is waiting! Yummy, yummy!" Dad was so silly.

As Brandon got up, so many thoughts were running through his head. He brushed his teeth and got dressed. "Did I really just meet a dragon named Eon? Did I really ride on his back and fly all over *Xiānggǎng* (香港)? It seemed so real."

Did Brandon really meet a dragon or was it just a dream?

CHAPTER 17

Going Home

(Friday)

Brandon couldn't believe the week was over—it went by like a flash! While he was stuffing clothes into his bag, *Gōnggong* (公公) walked in with a small sketchpad.

"Hi—*Hā luō* (哈囉), *Gōnggong* (公公)," Brandon said in his best Cantonese accent. "What's that—*Nà shì shénme* (那是什么)?"

Gōnggong (公公) handed Brandon the sketchpad without saying anything. Brandon opened it. On every page

Brandon Goes to Hong Kong (Xiānggǎng 香港)

was a drawing of a *lóng* (龙) that looked just like Eon.

"Wow! Who made these drawings, *Gōnggong* (公公)?" Brandon was trembling thinking that maybe last night's dream wasn't a dream after all.

"I did. When I was a boy, I often saw this *lóng* (龙). It was hard to describe so I started sketching it to show people to see if anyone else saw it. Unfortunately, no one else saw it and some thought I was making it up. After a while, I stopped seeing the *lóng* (龙), but I never forgot. To this day, I'm not sure if I had a wonderful imagination or I was special enough to see this magical *lóng* (龙)."

Brandon didn't know what to say. So many things were running through his mind. Finally, he asked, "So you believe in dragons?"

"I do," *Gōnggong* (公公) said with a twinkle in his eye.

"Then I do, too," said Brandon, and he began telling *Gōnggong* (公公) all about his dream, which maybe wasn't a dream after all! He told *Gōnggong* (公公) everything exactly as it had happened, without leaving out any details.

Gōnggong (公公) nodded throughout Brandon's rendition of last night's events. When Brandon finished he asked, "What do you think, *Gōnggong* (公公)? Do you think it really happened or do you think it was just a dream? It felt *really* real."

Gōnggong (公公) lips curled up in a smile and he shrugged. "It could be possible that it really happened. I think you must be extremely special for Eon to have chosen to appear to you and to have given you a tour of his *Xiānggǎng* (香港)."

Brandon hugged *Gōnggong* (公公) with all his might.

On the way to the airport, Brandon kept looking at the sketchpad *Gōnggong* (公公) had given him and thought of Eon. Although there was no proof or evidence of the existence of the great *lóng* (龙), Brandon liked believing in Eon and having this special bond with *Gōnggong* (公公) and Kelsey. He decided that they were lucky and special to be the only ones able to see and believe in this magical creature. And who knows? Maybe they weren't alone. Maybe there were others who could see and who believed, too.

Once the airplane took off, Brandon saw a red blur swoosh by. He just smiled. He was happy to believe that maybe, just maybe, there really was a big red *lóng* (龙), named Eon, flying around *Xiānggǎng* (香港), watching over its people.

What do you believe?

THE END

GLOSSARY

Locations/Attractions:

Běijīng (北京)—Beijing, the capital of China

Táiwān (台湾)—Taiwan

Xiānggǎng (香港)—Hong Kong

Zhōngguó (中国)—China

Family:

Gēge (哥哥)—Big brother

Gōnggong (公公)—Grandpa (mother's father), short for *wàigōng* (外公)—grandfather

Pópo (婆婆)—Grandma (mother's mother), short for *wàipó* (外婆)—grandmother

Other relatives not mentioned in this story:

Dìdi (弟弟)—Little brother

Jiějie (姐姐)—Big sister

Mèimei (妹妹)—Little sister

Brandon Goes to Hong Kong (Xiānggǎng 香港)

Nǎinai (奶奶)—Grandmother (Father's mother)

Yéye (爷爷)—Grandfather (Father's father)

People/Animals:

Nǐ (你)—You

Lóng (龙)—Dragon

Nǐmen (你们)—You all (plural)

Wǒ (我)—I or me

Wǒmen (我们)—We or us

Xióngmāo (熊猫)—Panda

Food/Meals:

Zǎofàn (早饭)—Breakfast

Wǔfàn (午饭)—Lunch

Wǎnfàn (晚饭)—Dinner

Bīngqílín (冰淇淋)—Ice cream

Diǎnxīn (点心)—Dim sum—small bite-sized portions of food served in small steamer baskets or on a small plate

Dòujiāng (豆浆)—Hot soybean broth

Jiǎozi (饺子)—Chinese dumplings

Yóutiáo (油条)—Strips of fried dough that look like a churros, but not sweet like churros—literally means, "oil strip". It is often dipped in *dòu jiāng* (豆浆).

Yúntūn miàn (云吞面)—Wonton noodle soup

Words/Phrases/Expressions:

Āiyō (哎哟)—Hey or wow (can also mean ouch)

Duìle (对了)—That's right; in Cantonese it's *deui liu*

Hā luō (哈囉)—Hello in Cantonese

Kāishǐle (开始了)—It's starting

Nà shì shénme (那是什么)?—What is that?

Nǐ hǎo (你好)—Hello; in Cantonese it's *néih hóu* (or *wèi* (喂) or *hā luō* (哈囉))

Shénme (什么)—What

Shì shénme (是什么)?—What is it?

Tài bàng le (太棒了)—How awesome

Brandon Goes to Hong Kong (Xiānggǎng 香港)

Wa (哇)—Wow

Wèi (喂)—Hi or hey in Cantonese

Xiè xiè (谢谢)—Thank you

Zài jiàn (再见)—Goodbye

Zěnme (怎么)—How

Zhēn de ma (真的吗)?—Really?

Zǒu ba (走吧)—Let's go

Languages:

Guǎngdōng huà (广东话)—Cantonese, a Chinese dialect spoken in Hong Kong and certain parts of China like Guangzhou

Pǔtōnghuà (普通话)—Mandarin, the official language of China

Yīngwén (英文)—English

Eugenia Chu

NOTES

You can find the following on my website at www.eugeniachu.com:

- Instructional video on Pinyin pronunciation and tones
- Audio of this book
- *Pópo's jiǎozi* (饺子) recipe
- Chinese character worksheets
- Dialogue discussing Cantonese and Chinese writing
- Plus a lot more!

If you liked this book, I would love, and be ever so grateful, if you would please post a review on Amazon. Your review not only helps others decide whether to buy this book, but will help to get this book noticed. Thank you!

ABOUT THE AUTHOR

Eugenia Chu is an attorney, turned stay-at-home mom, turned award winning and best selling children's book author. She is a first generation Chinese-American and lives in Miami with her husband and son, Brandon, who is the inspiration for her stories. She is also the author of *Brandon Makes Jiǎo Zi* (餃子), a picture book, and *Brandon Goes to Beijing* (北京), a chapter book. She has been a presenter at numerous schools in the US and abroad, libraries and book festivals.

When Brandon was very little, the author couldn't find children's storybooks to read to him which touched upon Chinese culture and which included some Chinese (Mandarin) words to teach and/or reinforce his Chinese vocabulary, so she started writing her own.

- www.eugeniachu.com
- www.amazon.com/author/eugeniachu
- www.goodreads.com/author/show/17045487.Eugenia_Chu
- @eugeniachu8245
- @chuauthor
- @eugeniachuauthor

ABOUT THE ILLUSTRATOR

Eliza Hsu Chen is an illustrator and graphic designer. Born to Taiwanese parents in Brazil, she was raised in Paraguay, and then moved to Miami when she was six. Her love for art grew during her years at Design and Architecture Senior High where she majored in architecture. She received the Posse scholarship and earned a bachelors in graphic design and marketing from Syracuse University.

In her downtime, she enjoys baking, food photography and visiting different cafés. She loves to travel all around the world and hopes to visit Hong Kong one day herself.

www.elizahsuchen.com

@eliza.hsu.chen

Made in the USA
Monee, IL
22 December 2024